Handbook of

Tanpura

HISTORY | ANATOMY | TUNING | MAINTENANCE

Handbook of
Tanpura

HISTORY | ANATOMY | TUNING | MAINTENANCE

By

Pankaj Vishal

PANKAJ PUBLICATIONS
New Delhi, INDIA

Handbook of Tanpura
First Published July, 2008
Copyright © Pankaj Publications

ISBN 13 :978-81-906139-2-7

Published by :
PANKAJ PUBLICATION
M-114, Vikas Puri
New Delhi 110 018
Email : contact@pankajmusic.com
       www.pankajmusic.com

Cover design by	:	Square vision
Typesetting by	:	Pankaj Books
Illustrations by	:	Mohit Suneja

Preface

ॐ ══════════════════════════ ॐ

The tradition of music in our country is as old as the civilization of this country itself. Music is considered to have a divine origin and one which brings its practitioner very close to God. But later it came to be presumed that music is an inborn quality, given by God Himself, and therefore, it can not be learned here on this earth. One may be trained in music and excel, provided there is genetic support. But, it is not a universal fact. One can learn everything with proper sincerity and devotion.

Keeping this in mind, we would like to introduce to the readers one of the most important instruments of Indian Music - the Tanpura. Although it is not meant for playing as a solo instrument, it certainly occupies a prominent place in the field of music - especially vocal. This is the reason that compelled us to familarize the readers with something more about this instrument.

This book gives a sound idea of the history, development and basics of the instrument to begin with, and then facilitates the reader in motivating his or her interest to know further and learn about this wonderful instrument.

This book takes care of the inquisitiveness of beginners and points out the salient problem areas of this field in a friendly and simple manner.

Any suggestions for improvement of this book are welcome.

PANKAJ VISHAL

Publishers' Note

ॐ ════════════════════════════════ ☙

The PANKAJ PUBLICATIONS is an undisputed leader and pioneer in the field of music books. The house is in continuous service to music lovers spread all over the world by promoting Indian music religiously by way of its books, C.D.s, journals and assisting practicing musicians.

A series of books with vital information about musical instruments, their origin, evolution, playing technique, etc. was in great demand for the last couple of years. In view of the larger interest of readers in general and music lovers in particular, we have brought this series of 'Handbooks' at the lowest possible price.

The entire editorial team of the PANKAJ PUBLICATIONS carried out intensive research and came out with fruits in the form of these books. We hope this series will be of immense help to people as our previous series of 'Pankaj Learn to play' proved to be.

If we are successful in our mission, although in a little way, the entire team along with this publication will be proud of the effort.

- *PUBLISHER*

Contents

ॐ ════════════════════════ ☙

Part - 1
The Tanpura -
Then & Now

The Tanpura

The Tanpura is an instrument which is inseparable from the Indian Music System, be it North Indian or Carnatic Music. It is a fretless instrument with four strings and a much sought after instrument in the musical arena. It plays a vital role in creating an aesthetic ambience on the stage which supports the musician with a musical background.

The tanpura constitutes a soundboard or *'Tabli'*, the gourd or *'Tumba'*, the neck heel or *'Gulu'* and a fingerboard. It is made from Tun wood but sometimes Teak is also used. The outer surface of the tanpura is well decorated to add beauty to its look.

The tanpura is a drone instrument, its literal meaning is *'Aadhar Swar'* or bass note. On it an artist enjoys the fullest possible freedom of exploring the different elements of music. But the work of the tanpura should not be confused with the specific note or rhythm. The tanpura produces a melodic background but not the melody; although the artist has full liberty to play it with a sense of rhythm. It follows a certain rhythmic structure.

The word "Tanpura" is a combination of two words. First is "Taan", which is of vital importance in music and refers to a particular aesthetical musical phrase and the second is "Pura", which means 'full' or 'complete'. Thus, literally the *Tanpura* implies completeness of music.

The tanpura gives support to all forms of music, be it vocal or instrumental. It crafts a musical continuity which any other string instrument, such as a Sitar or Sarod does not possess.

The special sound effect of the tanpura is achieved through its buzzing sound in which particular harmonics will resonate with focused clarity. Every string of the tanpura emits a wide spectrum of sound. Needless to say, for this the strings of the tanpura has to be attentively tuned to achieve a particular tonal shade and plucked by the fingers of the hand. There are many more things which are applied to get this effect, such as "*Javari*" and cotton threads, to fine tune the grazing contact to a different position on the *Javari* or bridge.

The tanpura has a hollow body which works as a soundbox for the instrument. When the strings of the tanpura are plucked a wave of vibrations are set up and it is conveyed to the resonator through the bridge and the resonating plank. The air cavity of the instrument amplify the projection of the basic tone.

Tanpuras, as we mentioned, are made up of tun wood or Teak wood. Tanpuras come in different sizes and with different names, such as bigger, smaller, male, female, instrumental and likewise. Generally there is a difference in a North Indian Tanpura and the one which is used in Carnatic Music. Here, the name too is different in the Carnatic style of Tanpura. These days there is another Tanpura which is electronic and very portable. Not only this, it does not require any person to play it. The tanpuras are designed in different styles, such as Miraj, Tanjore or Tamburi.

In a nut-shell, the tanpura, with the vibration of its strings creates a carpet of sound, not only as an accompaniment for traditional Indian Music but also for modal improvisations, overtone singing and musical meditation.

History & Development

History is always confusing and lacks in any sort of vital proof. Scholars remain busy for centuries to establish something of previous origin which inspires respect to our present culture.

First of all the a vital question arises. Why to go in search of answer to a question which is so ambiguous and to what purpose does it serve? The answer to this question is simple as the question itself. The lineage of a generation and part of ancient histroy fills us with a sense of pride. When we come to know that this is something that was once a part of our family, this attaches us to it automatically. And most importantly, when we are going to learn about something, we should be aware of its lineage, its evolution, development and all that which is connected to its origin. We should be aware under what circumstances the particular thing evolved from. Had the circumstance changed a little, what would have been the effect on it.

Therefore, before knowing anything further about the Tanpura, we would try to find out the circumstances, the place and the time when this instrument got its entry into this world, as it will motivate interest about it.

The tanpura is an instrument which is widely used in Indian Classical Music, although it is a part of Western Music in some parts of the world. But according to the appearance and temperament, this instrument is most suited for the Indian Music. Even then, we are not certain whether it actually got its birth in India or elsewhere. Indians never took pains to record their work of any nature, whether literature, religion, science or cultural. They just did their job and thats all. Therefore, we do not have any full proof idea or evidence of its origin.

That is why the origin of the Tanpura is highly disputed. Today it is generally believed that it is an instrument from Cental Asia.

A reference to the tanpura is found in the literature of the sixteenth and seventeenth centuries. Some believe that it developed with other instruments simultaneously at that time in Persia which is now Iran. But it is a secret that an instrument of foreign origin got its popularity and wide use in Indian Music. It is not clear and there is no evidence how it was Indianised in due course of time and came to serve as a drone instrument in the Indian Music System.

The tanpura is an instrument whcih is closely related to the 'leut' or the 'lute', with the Russian 'Balalaika', with the Ukrainian 'Bandura, the Italian 'Mandolin' and with the Spanish Guitar. It resembles so many other instruments which developed from the same origin in Central Asia. Twenty-three hundred years ago there was an instrument played by the Assyrians which was very close to the present day tanpura. The shape and appearance of it is very closely associated with two major instruments, the Sitar and Surbahar, which were prevalent in India for centuries.

There is no reliable data how the tambura came to its present form and use. To this day assumptions and ambiguity exist over it. But one thing is certain, that is, the tanpura did not get its birth in form as it looks today. It was the work of gradual development. It was not developed by a single person either. but in course of time it developed. Indians have a bigger and dominating role in its development because of its wide use in Indian music. Science can prove whether the tanpura was actually brought from Persia *(from the theory that Croats have Persian origin)*, or whether it was brought by the Turks to Bosnia or by someone else. One School here in India believes that the tanpura was invented and discovered in India alone as this is the country where drones are used so primarily and distinctly in its music system. But there is no certain evidence to prove this claim.

But according to most popular belief the tanpura was brought by Croats to their region. From there the instrument further migrated to all parts of Croatia and further to Hungary, Austria and Slovenia. According to this theory there is a possibility that the tanpura arrived in India with the Silk Route from Asia. But all these theories are based on the suggestive evidences only and no one is certain about its origin and development.

Later the tanpura underwent remarkable changes, developed and improved according to the taste of the music lovers of the world. The different shapes and sizes and use of different numbers of strings suggests that its development was gradual and slow but not static. Today too this instrument is under the process of research and development. In due course of time it is possible that the shape of the Tanpura may improve according to the convenience and the desired utility of music lovers. But it could be beyond doubt that the Tanpura will be an inseparable part of our music system as we have gotten accustomed to it.

Whatever may be the source or origin for such a wonderful instrument, which has given a new dimension to music in every corner of the world, let scholars debate on it. The only good thing for us in this regard is that there is a wonderful musical instrument for us to play and create an aesthetical musical circle.

We have tried our best to find its origin and place of development but since we are not able to say anything distinctly, let it be as it is. We only need to be grateful to the great masters who were part of this mega project.

Today this instrument has been accepted by all music lovers of the world. It is serving its purpose well by providing enrichness to the musical taste and here alone our purpose of looking back into its past is served.

There are different tuning styles prevalent in different corners of the world according to the desire and demand of music. The Tanpura gives support to musical concerts all over the world but as far as the Indian music is concerned, the role of the tanpura is tremendous. Likewise, there are different tuning styles in India also depending upon the notes of the *Ragas* to be sung or played. No concert or musical programme is complete without the participation of the tanpura as it's name suggests.

❋　❋　❋　❋

Drones in Indian Music

The drone is an essential part of traditional Indian music. It is found in classical music of both North and South India. Actually the drones are the vital part of music itself. Trying to find out the origin of the drone maybe confusing. The existance of music is as old as that of mankind. The sense of music must have been there in humans from its very appearance on this earth. It only took time to be manifested as humans became civilized. The use of drones in music is so evolved. Many percussion instruments are tuned in such a way as to reinforce the drone. Regardless of what provides the drone, it serves a vital function.

FUNCTION OF THE DRONE

The function of the drone is to provide a firm harmonic base for the music. It gives the musician a path to walk along and reach the highest attainable stage of musical perfection. A well tuned drone strings can produce all the seven notes of the octave. But the purpose of the drone is not to produce any note. Drones produce some notes as a base only. It produces a circle of certain pitches. The drone strings are tuned in a manner that emphasizes the tonic and the dominant notes of the *Raga*. When the drones are tuned this way the performer gets an opportunity to play with the melodies and build up a musical hollow.

The tonic in Western music is implicit in the scale structure. There are few modes used in Western music to identify the tonic. In Indian music numerous modes are used. These modes which are known as *Shrutis* are difficult to identify. This tonic sound reference helps the performer to identify *Shrutis*.

The continuous sounding of one or more notes provides the harmonic base for the performance. This not only clarifies the scale structure but actually makes it possible to develop amazingly complex modes. These modal explorations are possible because of subtle yet profound harmonic phenomena.

COMPONENTS OF THE DRONE

Indian drones use anything from a single note to all of the notes of the scale. The most simple drone consists of a single string as in an **Ektar**. When a single note drone is used it must be the **Sa** of the scale. Generally this type of drone is used in Folk Music. The drones could be made more complex by adding other notes to it. Both Hindustani and Carnatic Sangeet use two drones, the first and fifth notes of the scale. Many other combinations of the drone sounds are possible.

Ocassionally, drones can be more complex as there are in the tanpuras with four, five or six strings. Six and even seven-string tanpuras are available that provide far more than a simple *Sa-Pa* drone. The surmandal contains all the notes of the scale spread over several octaves. Although these lush drones are available, there is a tendency to use them judiciously; otherwise the performance may become muddy and the modes indistinct.

DRONES AND RHYTHM

Indian music displays a curious overlap between the drone accompaniment and rhythmic accompaniment. It is very normal for instruments or parts of instruments to be considered to provide either a rhythmic support or a drone. *Ektars* and *dotars* may be considered either drone instruments or rhythmic instruments because they perform both functions. The same can be said for the *chikari* strings of the Sitar or the *thalam* strings of the Veena. Even the Mridangam and the Tabla, which are considered by many to be the ultimate rhythmic instruments, continuously drone the tonic through the performance. We find that instruments whose only function is to drone (e.g., tanpura, surpeti) are few compared to the large number of instruments with dual functions. The player plucks the strings in a repetitive and continuous manner with a sense of rhythm and thus the drones provide the rhythm also.

THE DRONE AND THE RAGA

It is important for us to understand the use of drones with various north Indian *Ragas*. In *Hindustani Sangeet*, there is a tendency to think of the drone as a two-note musical device. The primary drone will be *(Sa)* and there will be one other note as the secondary drone. **Sa** cannot be eliminated from the drone. The secondary drone is selected according to the notes to be used in a *Raga*. Generally as a rule of thumb the fifth *(pancham)* is used, if not otherwise. In some *Ragas* where the *pancham* is not to be used *Madhyam* or *Nishad* is used.

CONCLUSION

Thus we can understand how the drones work and how important they are in Indian music. At first, the drone may appear to be trivial but it really is not. The drone is necessary to define the modality of the *Raga*. Sometimes this is very simple at other times it requires a rather sophisticated understanding of the structure of the *Raga*.

Indian String Instruments

Since we are dealing with an instrument with strings, it is important to know a little about other string instruments which are popular in India. A formal introduction to these instruments will help in understanding the spirit of the Tanpura.

According to ancient Indian scriptures, there was only one string instrument known as the 'Veena'. As we know from history most string instruments originated from the Veena, the combination of Iranian and middle eastern instruments to it divided the 'Veena' into two known types, these are **Tat** and **Vitat**, which literally means **Plucked** and **Unplucked,** respectively.

The **Tat** types of string instruments are either plucked or hammered. The Tanpura too comes in the category of plucked instruments as it is stroked on the strings by the fingers of the hand to produce sound. The **Tat** types of string instruments includes maximum number of instruments of lute and harp types such as :

1.	Sitar	8.	Ektar
2.	Rabab(Kabuli Rabab)	9.	Tanpura
3.	Sarod	10.	Dotar
4.	Saraswati Vina	11.	Santur
5.	Surbahar	12.	Surmandal
6.	Gotuvadyam	13.	Bulbul Tarang
7.	Rudra Vina	14.	Nakula Vina

15.	Vichitra Vina	18.	Magadi Vina
16.	Gettuvadyam	19.	Seni Rabab
17.	Gopichand (ektar)	20.	Sarangi

The next type is **Vitat**, which are bowed instruments. These are not traditionally known but a recent addition to the Indian music. These are such as:

1.	Saringda	5.Mayuri Vina
2.	Esraj	6.Sarangi
3.	Dilriba	7.Violin
4.	Chikara	

Out of these two types of plucked and bowed instruments some are not Indian instruments which are influenced by westernisation of music. But all the instruments have the capacity to play Indian rhythms and *Ragas*. The most popular amongst them remains to be the Sitar and Veena. The *Veena vadan* is less popular to be taken as 'too classical' because speed playing on the Veena is limited as compared to the sitar or the sarod. Not only this, some feel that the Sitar has more sweetness and better sound quality. Sitar playing gained popularity in the west because of its ease in playing and its rich tonal quality because of sympathetic strings.

The reason for the popularity of the above instruments named is they have the advantage of being played as solo instruments, which is not the case for the Tanpura.

The tanpura is not an instrument which can be played as a solo instrument like the Sitar or Sarod. Rather it is a supportive instrument. But the value of the tanpura rests in its capacity to provide drone accompaniment for performing artists, be it vocal or instrumental. As described above we have come to know that without the help of the tanpura no Indian concert is complete. It is so important that we can not imagine serious music without the participation of the tanpura.

It is worth mentioning here that the shape of the tanpura resembles greatly to the sitar and surbahar or veena. It gives ample proof of its origin in India as so many scholars believe that it is an instrument that was born in Central Asia.

✳ ✳ ✳ ✳

Part – 2
Theory of Music

The Indian Music System

Indian Music is based on *Ragas* and *Ragas* are based on *the Nadas, Shrutis, Swaras, Saptaka* and *Thaats*, as shown in the evolution chart.

Nada (Sound) : This is sound produced by striking, friction or beating. *'Nada'* is of two kinds:

(a) *Sangeet-un-upyogi Nada* **(Non-Musical sound)***:* Those sounds which are not musical such as machine rattlings, traffic horns, shouting etc. These sounds are not pleasant to listen to and are disturbing in nature. They can cause headaches and irritation. We hear these sounds in our day-to-day lives in the city.

(b) *Sangeet-upyogi Nada* **(Musical sound):** Contrary to non-musical sounds, these sounds are pleasant to listen to and musically audible. These can be the sounds of nature as the chirping of birds, water falls, flowing river, singing etc. These sounds are relaxing and give a feeling of tranquility and peace. Musical sounds like singing and instrumental playing have the virtue to hypnotize an audience.

Shruti **(Microtonal Interval notes)**: These are microtonal sounds found between **Sangeet-upyogi Nadas** (musical sounds). They can be heard and distinguished by a sensitive musical ear only. They can now be seen visually on an 'Oscilloscope'. *Shrutis* are also called Microtonal Intervals of Sound. The gaps are increased between the sounds to make these **Shrutis** to **notes** for the purpose of easy recognition and the development of music by using them when playing and singing.

25

There are 22 *Shrutis* used in Indian Music.

1. Tivra	8. Raudri	15. Rakta
2. Kumudwati	9. Krodhi	16. Sandipini
3. Manda	10. Vajrika	17. Alapini
4. Chhandovati	11. Prasarini	18. Madanti
5. Dayawati	12. Priti	19. Rohini
6. Ranjani	13. Manjari	20. Romya
7. Raktika	14. Kshiti	21. Ugra
		22. Kshobhini

Swaras (Notes): *Swaras* (notes) are produced by *Shrutis* with big intervals or Gaps. They can be distinguished by the ears of listeners. The difference between 'Swaras' and 'Shrutis' is that the 'Swaras' are measured by *Shrutis* depending on the intervals or number of *Shrutis*.

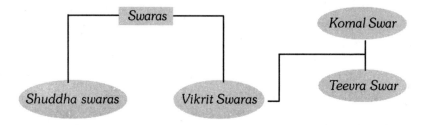

Swaras are of two types, *Vikrits* **Swara (Distorted note)** and **Shuddha Swara (Full Tone note)**

Shuddha Swaras (Full Tone Notes). These are natural notes which are found in the *Shrutis*. To recognize the minute gap of *Shrutis* easily.

Shudha Swaras or Full Tone Notes were identified and called **Natural notes** and they are 7 of them.

Vedic names along with the popular short names of these 7 notes are given below. The complete music theory is based on these 7 notes and their combinations.

S. No.	Name of Swaras	Shuddha Swaras	Western Notes	Shruti
1.	Shadaj	Sa	C	4 Tivra, Kumudwati, Manda Chhandovati.
2.	Rishabh	Re	D	3 Dayawati, Ranjani, Raktika
3.	Gandhar	Ga	E	2 Raudri & Krodhi
4.	Madhyam	Ma	F	4 Vajrika, Prasarini, Priti, Manjari
5.	Pancham	Pa	G	4 Kshiti, Rakta, Sandipini Alapini
6.	Dhaiwat	Dha	A	3 Madanti, Rohini, Romya
7.	Nishad	Ni	B	2 Ugra Kshobhini

With the identification of these full tone notes the gap between the notes becomes wider. The wider the gap the greater the obstruction to the sweetness of sound. Musicians then introduced **Half Tone Notes** or **Flat Notes** (*Komal Swaras*) between two **Full Tone Notes** (*Shuddha Swaras*), and thus **Distorted notes** (*Vikrit Swaras*) came into existance.

Vikrit Swaras **(Distorted Notes)** : *Vikrit Swaras* are of two types, they are *Komal Swaras* (Flat Notes or Half Tone Notes) and *Tivra Swara* (Sharp note). With the introduction of the distorted notes, *Sa* and *Pa* though remained unchanged.

Komal Swaras **(Flat notes or Half Tone Notes)** are found between two **shudha swaras (Full Tone *notes*)**. These *Swaras* are a bit lower in pitch from the *Shuddha Swaras*. They are symbolized in notation by a Dash (_) below the note such as **Re**. A half step lower.

✌ There are four *Komal Swaras* (flat notes). These are: **Re, Ga, Dha, & Ni.**

Tivra Swar is the note which appears a half step above the full note and is called a **sharp note (*Tivra Swar*).** This *Swar* (note) is higher in pitch from the *Shuddha Swara*. It is symbolized in notation by a small vertical line (') over the note.

✌ There is only one *Tivra Swar,* which is **Ma**.

According to two different notation systems, it is important to understand the difference between the two. There are two fixed notes in Indian system. These are **Sa** & **Pa.** The remaining five notes have two different types as semitone or distorted forms. On the other hand there are two types for all the seven notes in the western system. There is a distortion of each note and all the notes can be either flat or sharp. The closest related western note to the Indian distorted notes are as follows -

Indian Notes	Re	Ga	Ma	Dha	Ni
Western Notes	$C^\#$ or D^b	$D^\#$ or E^b	$F^\#$ or G^b	$G^\#$ or A^b	$A^\#$ or B^b

1. As shown in the table, note **komal Re** is shown as it is but in western system, it is written as two types, either **C#** or **D**. Where (**#**) symbol is used for sharp (*tivra*) and (♭) symbol is used for flat (*komal*).

2. There are two fixed notes in the Indian system. These are **Sa** & **Pa**, which cannot be changed to flats or sharp.

3. Western music does not have sharp for note **E** & **B**. Instead, **F** stands for **E#**, and **C** stands for **B#**.

This is how the Twelve notes come to exist. They are as follows.

Sl. No.	Swaras	Description	Western Name
1.	**Sa**	*Shudha* **(Fixed)**	**C Fixed**
2.	Re	*Komal*	D Half Tone note
3.	**Re**	*Shuddha*	**D Full tone note**
4.	Ga	*Komal*	E Half tone note
5.	**Ga**	*Shuddha*	**E Full tone note**
6.	**Ma**	*Shudha*	**F Full tone note**
7.	Ma	*Tivra*	F Sharp note
8.	**Pa**	*Shuddha* **(Fixed)**	**G Fixed**
9.	Dha	*Komal*	A Half tone note
10.	**Dha**	*Shuddha*	**A Full note**
11.	Ni	*Komal*	B Half Tone note
12.	**Ni**	*Shuddha*	**B Full Note**

A group of these 7 Natural Notes (*Shuddha Swaras*) make a *Saptak* (Octave). The *Saptak* also includes 4 *Komal* and one *Tivra Swar*. In all there are 12 Notes to make a complete **Saptak (Octave).** A *Saptak* (Octave) includes the *guru* notes of Indian Music which are **Sa Re Ga Ma Pa Dha Ni.** A specific combination of these *Swar*as (Notes) from the *Saptak* forms a **Thaat (scale),** which is the basis of the *Ragas*.

Ragas (Melodies) are a particular combination of these notes or group of notes, which are produced from **Thaats (scales).**

In a nutshell, we can understand the journey of swaras from its origin to Nada by this evolution chart.

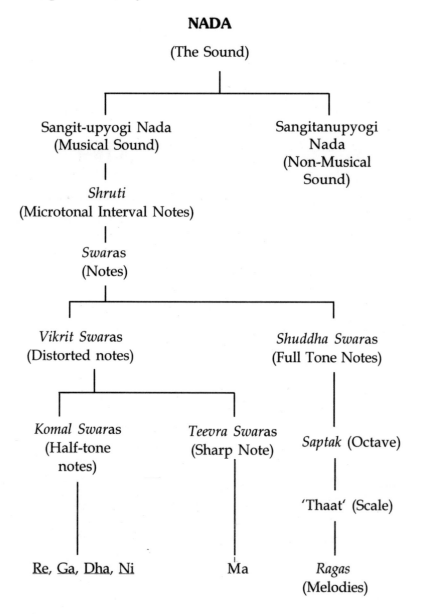

NADA

(The Sound)

Sangit-upyogi Nada
(Musical Sound)

Sangitanupyogi Nada
(Non-Musical Sound)

Shruti
(Microtonal Interval Notes)

*Swar*as
(Notes)

*Vikrit Swar*as
(Distorted notes)

*Shuddha Swar*as
(Full Tone Notes)

*Komal Swar*as
(Half-tone notes)

*Teevra Swar*as
(Sharp Note)

Saptak (Octave)

'Thaat' (Scale)

Re, Ga, Dha, Ni

Ma

Ragas
(Melodies)

SAPTAK (Octave)

According to the Indian theory of music there are three ranges of the human voice, which are low, medium and high pitch. These pitches when identified with notes in music called *Saptaka* or a group of seven *Shuddha* notes. These seven notes also includes four *komal* and one *Tivra Swara*. The human voice is differentiated under these three ranges:

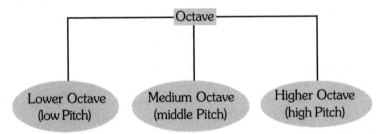

1. **Madhya Saptaka** (Medium Octave) — When the sound naturally comes out of the throat without any pressure, it is called the throat voice. The Medium octave or *Madhya Saptaka*.

2. **Mandra Saptaka** (Lower Octave) — When the sound comes out entirely by the pressure of the lungs, it is called the chest voice or *Mandra Saptaka* (Lower Octave). In this *Saptaka* the pitch of the sound is lower than the medium octave.

3. **Tar Saptaka** (Upper Octave) — When the sound is produced with the exertion of force on the nostrils and head, called the head voice or *Tar Saptaka* (Upper Octave). The pitch or sound is higher than that of the medium octave.

THAAT

Ordinarily a *Thaat* is a combination of **seven Swaras** or notes capable of producing *Ragas*. All the notes played in *thaat* are in ascending order starting from **Sa** ending at **Ni,** whether natural, flat or sharp. There are basically ten *thaats* in Indian music system.

The *Thaat* must qualify these three Basic conditions :

1. A *Thaat* must contain the seven *swaras* (notes) in the regular form.

2. The *Shuddha*, *Komal* or *Tivra Swaras* must appear one after the other.

3. It is a mere scale, a combination of notes. It does not essentially need to please the listeners ear.

Ten thaats and their notes as follows:

1.	Bilawal	Sa	Re	Ga	Ma	Pa	Dha	Ni
2.	Khamaj	Sa	Re	Ga	Ma	Pa	Dha	<u>Ni</u>
3.	Kafee	Sa	Re	<u>Ga</u>	Ma	Pa	Dha	<u>Ni</u>
4.	Asawari	Sa	Re	<u>Ga</u>	Ma	Pa	<u>Dha</u>	<u>Ni</u>
5.	Bhairav	Sa	<u>Re</u>	Ga	Ma	Pa	<u>Dha</u>	Ni
6.	Kalyan	Sa	Re	Ga	Ḿa	Pa	Dha	Ni
7.	Poorvi	Sa	<u>Re</u>	Ga	Ma	Pa	<u>Dha</u>	Ni
8.	Bhairavi	Sa	<u>Re</u>	<u>Ga</u>	Ma	Pa	<u>Dha</u>	<u>Ni</u>
9.	Todi	Sa	<u>Re</u>	<u>Ga</u>	Ḿa	Pa	<u>Dha</u>	Ni
10.	Marva	Sa	<u>Re</u>	Ga	Ma	Pa	Dha	Ni

RAGAS

A *Raga* is a combination of sounds or *swaras* having qualities that give pleasure to the listener. Every *Raga* has a peculiar quality of its own. To be acquainted with *Ragas,* a musician should bear in mind the following points :

1. *Ragas* must belong to a *Thaat.*

2. At least five notes are essential for a *Raga.*

3. In a *Raga* the melody is very essential.

4. A *Raga* must have its own ascent, descent (*Aroha* and *avaroha*) and fixed notes *(Vadi & Samvadi).*

5. The **Sa** *Swara* (C note) is the same note (fixed) in every *Raga*, and both **Ma** & **Pa** are not to be omitted at the same time.

Parts of combination of a raga

There are 4 distinguished parts of a raga/composition/song.

1. Sthayi   :   First part (face) or introduction.

2. Antara   :   Second part or body.

3. Sanchari   :   Combinarion of notes of 'Sthayi' & 'Antara'.

4. Abhog   :   Some notes of the composition played in the upper octave.

Categories of Ragas (*Jati' of a Raga*)

The following are the three most common categories of Ragas :

1. **Sampurna** has seven notes ascending and descending.

2. **Shadava** has six notes ascending and descending.

3. **Odava** has five notes in the same *Swaras*, both ascending & descending.

Categories of Ragas

S. No.	Category	No. of Swaras		Total No. of Ragas with the Combination of Ascending & Descending Notes
		Ascent	Descent	
1.	Sampurna–Sampurna	7	7	1 – 1 x 1 – 1
2.	Shadava–Shadava	6	6	6 – 6 x 6 – 36
3.	Odava–Odava	5	5	15 – 15x15– 225
4.	Sampurna–Shadava	7	6	6 – 1 x 6 – 6
5.	Sampurna–Odava	7	5	15 – 1 x 15 – 15
6.	Shadva–Sampurna	6	7	6 – 6 x 1 – 6
7.	Shadva–Odava	6	5	90 – 6 x 15 – 90
8.	Odava–Sampurna	5	7	15 – 15 x 1 – 15
9.	Odava–Shadava	5	6	90 – 15 x 6 – 90

Lay (Tempo or Speed)

LAY : (Tempo)

In the ordinary sense *lay* means Beat or speed or any regular space of time between boundaries to complete a circle in a specific time period. It is a natural harmonious flow of vocal and instrumental sound with a regular succession of accents. There is no fixed structure of speed or tempo in music. Every musician chooses it according to his convenience; but basically, what is important is that one should be able to control the *lay* or tempo of *taal*. The tempo should neither be too slow nor should it be extraordinarily fast. Not only this, even in a slow tempo it should be in such a manner that it can entertain the audience on the one hand and on the other its musicality will not be sacrificed.

Normally a slow tempo should be half the tempo of a standard one and a fast tempo should be double that of the standard. But again it differs according to the capabilitiy of the musician. An expert musician starts the tempo in a very slow pace and gradually increases it reaching the required speed.

According to observations there are mainly three types of beat which have been accepted in the Indian music. But there is one more special type called '*Ati Drut Lay*', which is generally used by expert musicians, because tempo in this particular type is very fast and very tough to control. All percussion instruments are used to control and regularize the musical sound.

The Three types of beats are :

1. **Madhya Lay** (Medium or Normal Beat).
   eg. 1 2 3 4

2. **Drut Lay** (Quick or Fast Beat).
   eg. 1 2 3 4

3. **Vilambit Lay** (Slow Beat).
   eg. 1   2   3   4

(Note the space between the numbers)

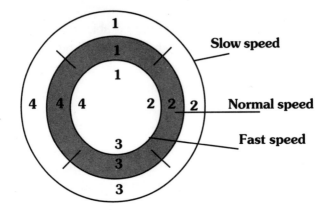

Normal Tempo

Normal Beat is the time required by a musician to complete a round or a part of a song, tune or dance in a comfortable speed without any stress. Although no fix structure is available for this, convenience is the key. The tempo should be easy enough within the musician's control. In a normal speed any composition whether instrumental or vocal leaves a very refreshing effect on the audience. The Normal beat is the basis of the remaining two beats.

Eg. 1 2 3 4 1 2 3 4 etc.

Fast Tempo

Fast Beat means half the time of a normal beat. This is when a musician, say, requires one minute of time to complete a part of a song, tune or dance, in normal beat, now he will require half the time taken by the normal beat. In other words we can say that the musician can take two rounds of his play for the time required in the normal beat.

Eg. 1 2 3 4-1 2 3 4-1 2 3 4 etc.

Slow Tempo

In Slow Beat a musician takes double the time to complete the round required by the medium or normal beat. Suppose if he completes a round of his song in one minute in normal beat, he will now take two minutes to complete the same song.

Eg. 1 - 2 - 3 - 4 - 1 - 2 - 3 - 4   etc.

Comparative speeds in various beats:

Slow beat	:	1			2			3			4		
Medium Beat	:	1	2	3	4	1	2	3	4				
Fast Beat	:	1 2 3 4	1 2 3 4	1 2 3 4	1 2 3 4	1 2 3 4							

Taal (The Rhythm)

Taal or Rhythm is the regular succession of sound vibrations, necessary to make sound musical. It is a scale for producing the rhythmic pattern in a song or *Raga*. Each song or composition runs on a particular time scale, and the scale is repeated in a particular gap, this gap is repeated for a specific number of times, which makes the rhythm cycle for the composition. The gaps between the notes in a scale is known as intervals, which can be created by clapping, or by a percussion instrument. The most popular is the Tabla. The early Indian musicians invented many *taals* of different *matras* (Rhythms), *Khand* (Bars) and *Bols* (Sounds) and fixed the points of 'Sam', *Talis* and *Khalis* for every *Taal*.

Beat : As we know well now, beat is a time-scale map in a composition. The common beats in the Indian system are *Kehrava Taal* (8 beats) and *Daadara taal* (6 beats).

Beat and its part in a composition is written and understood by some technical names like *sam, tali, khali*, etc. in the Indian music system. These terms and names carry a lot of importance for the beginners to understand. Let's learn them in detail.

Bol (Sounds) : Each beat is made out of notes or sounds. These sounds can be of percussions or of melody notes. The sounds created by percussions like drums or tabla, played as accompaniment or are spoken as **Dha, Dhin,** etc. are known as Bols.

Sam : The starting point of a taal notation or a beat cycle, from the point where the beat starts in a composition is known as **Sam.** This is the point in a notation where all the instruments stops and start together when playing many instruments together. It is shown in the notation with **(x)** sign.

Taali : Literally means the clap, it is the particular point in a notation where maximum pressure is given to the playing. This is also the repeated starting point of a part in a beat cycle.

For example; as shown below, while playing "*Teen Taal*" 1st, 5th, & 13th bol has *taali* in its place -

Beat signs	×				2			
Beat	1	2	3	4	5	6	7	8
Bol	Dha	Dhin	Dhin	Dha	Dha	Dhin	Dhin	Dha
Beat signs	0				3			
Beat	9	10	11	12	13	14	15	16
Bol	Dha	Tin	Tin	Ta	Ta	Dhin	Dhin	Dha

Khali : Khali literally means empty space, which is actually not, only the force or emphasis of sound is less in this part. *Khali* in a composition means a gap of some *matras* within *boles* of *Theka* played by the right hand on the Tabla only while the left (*Duggi* or *Dhama*) remains silent in *khali matra* time. This is a point in a notation where comparatively less force is given to the *bol*. For example, while playing "*teen taal*", the 9th beat in the cycle is the space for *khali*.

Parts: Putting all the sounds in a group separated by *sam*, *tali* and *khali* are known as parts or measures. Parts are shown in notation by a vertical line between the group of notes or sounds. For example: *Daadra taal* is of two parts with 3 sounds per measure:

Beat signs	×			0		
Beat	1	2	3	4	5	6
Bol	Dha	Dhin	Na	Ta	Tin	Na

All the symbols such as *sam, tali khali* are placed on the 1st note of the group.

Sthayi : First part or the introduction of the song or a composition which is repeated in the song after paragraphs is called *sthayi*.

Antara : The second part or the middle part of the song which is also known as the body is called *Antara*.

Some Important Beats

Keherva Taal

It is the most popular and common *Taal* used in Indian Light Music. It has 8 '*matras*' or beat with **sam** on the 1st beat and **khali** on the 5th. *Ghazal* and *Bhajan* & Light music get beautiful expression in this *taal*. This *taal* is relatively easy to learn and understand and therefore very popular among musicians.

Parts/Measures - 2   Beats - 8
one taali & one Khali

Beat signs	x				0			
Beat	1	2	3	4	5	6	7	8
Bol	Dha	Ge	Na	Ti	Na	Ka	Dhi	Na

Dadra Taal

This is another popular *taal* of Indian Light Music. It consists of 6 *matras* with *sam* on the 1st and *khali* on 5th. Any composition of '*Sringar Ras*' will suit this *taal*. Generally *Thumri*, *Bhajans* and *Ghazals* are sung in this *taal*. This *taal* is very easy to grasp and learn, therefore it is very much in use in the field of music.

Parts/Measures - 2   Beats - 6
one taali & one Khali

Beat signs	×			0		
Beat	1	2	3	4	5	6
Bol	Dha	Dhin	Na	Dha	Tin	Na

Roopak Taal

One of the most popular *taals* of Indian Music; used both in light as well as classical music. It has 7 beats with *sam* on the 1st and *taali* on 5th & 7th *matras*. Some musicians believe that *khali* is on the 1st. Classical compositions as well as light *bhajans* and *ghazals* are made to flourish in this *taal* very extensively. Being a *taal* of odd numbers it is very impulsive and its least numbers of beat make it easier to grasp and control.

Parts/Measures - 3   Beats - 7
Two taali & one Khali

Beat signs	×			2		3	
Beat	1	2	3	4	5	6	7
Bol	Tin	Tin	Na	Dhin	Na	Dhin	Na

(**Note** : Roopak taal starts from sam, so the taali is not given there.)

Deep Chandi Taal

This *taal* is usually used in classical music only. It has 14 beats with *sam* on the 1st. This *taal* is generally used by expert musicians. Although light composition can be sung or played in this *taal* but it is not so easy to handle. Medium tempo compositions are used in this *taal*.

Parts/Measures - 4   Beats - 14
Three taali & one Khali

Beat signs	×			2			
Beat	1	2	3	4	5	6	7
Bol	Dha	Dhin	S	Dha	Dha	Tin	S
Beat signs	0			3			
Beat	8	9	10	11	12	13	14
Bol	Ta	Tin	S	Dha	Dha	Dhin	S

Teen Taal

This is the base of all *taals* in Indian Music. It has 16 beats with *sam* on 1st, 2nd taali on 5th, *khali* on 9th and 3rd *taali* on 13th. It is called base of all taals because every other *taal* is in the fraction of *teen taal*. It is easy to learn and most widely used in music both light and classical. Slow and medium and fast compositions are played and sung in this *taal*.

Parts/Measures - 4   *Beats - 16*
Three taali & one Khali

Beat signs	×				2			
Beat	1	2	3	4	5	6	7	8
Bol	Dha	Dhin	Dhin	Dha	Dha	Dhin	Dhin	Dha
Beat signs	0				3			
Beat	9	10	11	12	13	14	15	16
Bol	Dha	Tin	Tin	Ta	Ta	Dhin	Dhin	Dha

Jhap Taal

This *taal* too is very popular but mostly used in classical music. it has 10 matras with *sam* on 1st and 2nd *taali* on 5th, *khali* on 9th and 3rd *taali* on 10th. Composition in slow and medium tempo is generally used in this *taal*. Although light compositions can be made in this *taal* but generally it is not because its rhythm pattern is somewhat different and not so easy to learn and grasp compared to other *taals*.

Parts/Measures - 4   *Beats - 10*
Three taali & one Khali

Beat signs	×		2		0			3		
Beat	1	2	3	4	5	6	7	8	9	10
Bol	Dhin	Na	Dhin	Dhin	Na	Tin	Na	Dhin	Dhin	Na

Ek Taal

One of the popular *taals* of Indian music system. This *taal* is used in classical music but may be used in light music also. It has 12 *matras* with *sam* on the 1st beat. Slow and fast tempo compositions are used in this *taal*. This *taal* has three times the beat that of *Dadra taal* and hence its rhythm pattern is similar to the later. This *taal* is easy to learn and grasp and is impulsive in nature.

Parts/Measures - 6   Beats - 12
Four taali & Two Khali

Beat signs	×		0		2	
Beat	1	2	3	4	5	6
Bol	Dhin	Dhin	DhaGe	TirKit	Tu	Na
Beat signs	0		3		4	
Beat	7	8	9	10	11	12
Bol	Kat	Ta	DhaGe	TirKit	Dhin	Na

Teevra Taal

It is also a popular and old *taal* of Indian music system. Initially it was played on pakhawaj only but now it is widely played in tabla also. Similar to *Roopak* this *taal* has 7 beats. This *taal* is used in classical music only in medium or slow tempo. Its nature is very intense and therefore is used in serious music such as *Dhrupad* and *khayal* etc.

Parts/Measures - 3   Beats - 7
Three taali

Beat signs	×			2		3	
Beat	1	2	3	4	5	6	7
Bol	Dha	Din	Ta	Tit	Kat	GaDe	Gin

Indian Music Notation System

Tips to Read a Composition

1. **Shudha Swaras (Full tone Notes):** No sign is required i.e. Sa. Re, Ga, Ma, Pa, Dha, Ni. Only the first letter is required in the notation i.e. S, R, G, M, P, D, N.

2. **Komal Swaras (Half Tone Notes):** A dash (—) is written under the notes i.e. R G D N.

3. **Tivra Swara (Sharp Note):** A small perpendicular line is placed over the note i.e. M.

4. **Madhya Saptak Swaras (Medium Octave Notes):** No sign is required for this octave notes i.e. S R G M P D N.

5. **Mandra Saptak Swaras (Lower Octave Notes):** A dot is written under the notes i.e. S R G M P D N

6. **Ati Mandra Saptak Swaras (Double lower octave):** Two dots are written under the notes i.e. S P

7. **Tar Saptak Swaras (Upper Octave Notes):** A dot is written over the notes S R G M P D N

8. **Matras** are shown in numbers 1 2 3 4 5 6 etc. Normally one note shows one *Matra* time.

9. **Tali:** Numbers written between the bars.

10. **Khali:** A Zero (0) is shown in a bar.

11. **Sam:** A sign of (×) is written on the first matra of every *Taal*.

44

12. **Khand (Bar):** Vertical lines drawn indicating divisions of *Taals*.

13. **Extending or prolonging** of Notes, a dash (—) is written after the notes. One dash shows one matra time.

	1st Khand		2nd Khand		3rd Khand
	Sam	Tali	Khali		Tali
	×	2	0		3
Matras	1 2 3 4	5 6 7 8	9 10 11 12		13 14 15 16

14. Two, Three or Four notes in a ***matra*** time. These notes are combined together by a bracket under the notes i.e. SR SRG SRGM

15. **Jhala (Vamping):** To express *Jhala* normally "*J*" sign is used. But traditionally and mostly a space is mentioned (–) as *jhala* with notes.

16. **Meend:** Meend is shown by a semicircular line over the notes i.e. SG SM SP.

17. **Chikari:** Small (c) is written after the note. i.e. Sc, Rc,Gc.

18. **Kan Swara (Grace note):** Small letter is written in superscript by the side of the main note on the right.

M^G P^M

19. **Prolonging, Pause or Extending the note length:** Dashes are placed after a note, one dash is fixed for one matra time.

i.e. S—, R— —,G— —.

Western Notation System

The Western notation system is based on time symbols and where they are placed on the staff. These signs show both the *Swaras* and the length of time. These symbols are the notes, written on a set of 5 horizontal lines and 4 equal spaces between them called the Staff. There are two sets of the staff on which music notes are written: one for the lower tones or sounds and the other for the higher tones or sounds. The **lower tones or pitches** are represented by the **Bass** (*pronounced base*) **Staff** on which the Bass Clef Sign (𝄢) is written and the **higher tones or pitches** and **medium tones or pitches** are represented by the **Treble Staff** on which the Treble clef sign (𝄞) is written. Together these two staves make the **Grand Staff.**

The symbols of notes used in western music and their near meanings in Indian Music are given below.

Symbols of Notes		Sound Values
Whole Note or Semi-breve	𝅝	4 beats)*Matra*) of sound
Half Note or Minim	𝅗𝅥	2 beats (*Matra*) of sound
Quarter Note or Crotchet	𝅘𝅥	1 beat (*Matra*) of sound
Dotted Half Note or Dotted Minim	𝅗𝅥.	3 beats (*Matra*) of sound
Eighth Note or Quaver	𝅘𝅥𝅮	½ beat (*Matra*) of sound
16th Note or Semi-quaver	𝅘𝅥𝅯	¼ (*Matra*) beat of sound

Symbols of Notes		Sound Values
Full Tone Notes or Naturals	♮	Shudh Swaras (denoted as SRGMPDN)
Half Tone Notes or Flats	♭	Komal Swaras (denotes with line under the note: S <u>RG</u> MP <u>DM</u>)
Sharp Note	♯	Tivra Swara (denote with a vertcal line over the note; SRGM̌PDN
Bass Cleff sign	𝄢	Mandra Saptaka (denote with a '•' under the note; S R G M P D N
Treble Cleff sign	𝄞	Tar saptak (denote with a '•' over the notes: S R G M P D N

Apart from the above symbols in western music the beat is also very important. In fact it is the backbone of all music. Without the beat there is no music. The beat in music is related to Time which is Space between measuring units which are numbers. Without numbers we cannot measure time or any form of measurement for that matter. Hence Time maybe defined as space between numbers. So also the beat in music which is *Equal spaces of time between numbers*. These spaces must be equal in music otherwise it is just noise. This means if we have a piece of music that has four beats

the 1st beat will be the **space** between numbers 1 and 2

the 2nd beat will be the **space** between numbers 2 and 3

the 3rd beat will be the **space** between numbers 3 and 4, and

the 4th beat will be the **space** between numbers 4 and 1.

Unlike Indian music western music does not have a **0 beat**, which is called **Khali**. Western music starts on the 1st beat.

The symbols which represent the sounds are called notes. They have sound values to them. When written on the staff, the note symbols represent the different lengths of sound, thus, making the rhythm of music. Rhythm may then be defined as the combination of all the long and short sounds in a piece of music within a specific beat. In other words the combination of all the different kinds of notes in a piece of music. There are basically four types of Rhythm from which all music is written. These are as follows:

1. A rhythm where the sound is more than one beat (single space of time) or in other words a note represents two or more beats of sound.

2. A rhythm where the sound is equal to one beat (single space of time) or a note represents one beat of sound.

3. A rhythm where the single beat (single space of time) will have two sounds which means that the beat is divided into two sounds which are equal in length.

4. A rhythm where the single beat (space of time) will have three or four or more sounds within the beat and these are also equally divided.

Western music is also divided into sections or divisions which we call Measures which are formed by vertical lines on the staff which we call Bar Lines. The beat in western music is grouped normally in double, triple, or quadruple time that is 2, 3 or 4 beats per measure. We find this in the time signature which is a set of two numbers one above the other. These numbers are normally found in the beginning of a piece of music.

Just as we speak in sentences to make sense in music we also have musical sentences which we call phrases and which normally consist of four measures of sound but which may also vary depending on the composition. These musical sentences are marked by curved lines called Slurs. These lines are found over a set of notes on the staff which indicate the phrase of music which expresses an idea. A complete sentence would normally consists of two phrases, the first called the **statement** and the second the **response**. These musical phrases or sentences usually end in a form of punctuation which we call **cadences** in music. They denote the end of a phrase.

All music is based on scales hence scales are the skeleton or backbone of any musical composition. In western music we have two basic kinds of scales - the Major scales and the Minor scales. The Minor scales are of three types - these are Natural minor, the Harmonic minor and the Melodic minor scales. Scales are built on a pattern of Tones and semitones. These tones and semitones are the distances of sounds. The semitones are the closest distance of two notes or pitches while the tones are two semitones side by side. Basing on the pattern of tones and semitones scales are identified as whether they are sharp scales or flat scales. A **sharp scale** is when the natural note of the scale is *raised* by a semitone and a **flat scale** is when the natural note of the scale is *lowered* by a semitone.

For example:
G major the notes are G A B C D E F$^\sharp$ G
F major the notes are   F G A B$^\flat$ C D E F

All together we have about sixty scales in western music, these include all the majors and their relative minors, in all 3 forms. The **number of sharps or flats** in them we call the **key signature** of a scale. This includes the three types of minor scales as mentioned earlier. One may compare scales to multiplication tables in school which need to be learnt if we want to understand music properly. They are most essential in music learning.

Another very important aspect of western music is the skill of reading music which is most important if one is to be a good musician. For this we learn to identify **notes** on the staff, that is the lines and spaces, by the *distances* between them as they are *written on the staff,* up or down the staff. We call this Intervals between notes. We know that there are eight notes to a scale hence we number them as 1 2 3 4 5 6 7 8 or call them the eight degrees of a scale. Basing on this we identify the intervals between notes written on the lines and spaces. The following are the intervals identified.

1. Repeat - This is the interval of notes on the same line or space on the staff.

eg. Notes on the same second line or same third space.

2. Second - (Step) - The interval from a line note to a space note up or down.

eg. Notes on the 1st line and the 1st space up or notes on the 4th space and 4th line down.

3. Third - (Skip) - The interval from a line note to the next line note or from a space note to the next space note up or down.

eg. 3rd line note to 4th line note up or 2nd space note to 1st space note down.

4. Fourth - (3rd + 2nd) - The interval from a line note to a space note or space note to a line note up or down with a space and line in between.

eg. 1st line note to 2nd space note up or 4th line note to 2nd space note down.

5. Fifth - (3rd + 3rd) - The interval from a line note to a line note or space note to a space note up or down with a line or space in between.

eg. 1st line note to 3rd line note up or 3rd space note to 1st space note down.

Interval reading helps in getting the right pitch (sound) and the correct finger to play on the instrument. This skill of reading is most helpful for a smooth flowing production of sound on any instrument.

Points To Remember for Combined Notation System

Before using combined notation system the musicians should bear the following points in mind.

1. **The middle point C is fixed for every song, *Raga* or tune. The Sa or C note is compulsory. All tunes are based on the C note.**

2. **G note [P] cannot be changed into a half tone (flat) or a sharp note.**

3. **P and F cannot be omitted at a time in any *Raga*.**

The Symbol of *matra* on the staff notation is accepted by our combined notation system. It is equal to one *matra* time. Symbols of No.1 and No.2 are not used in combined notation system. The remaining fractional *matra* time symbols may be used as they are. The position of symbol of time notes in the clefs are accepted as they are.

Symbols of half tone notes (flats) and the sharp note are accepted. The symbol of extension of sound [—] is accepted for prolonging the notes, not for ending the sound. This symbol denotes one *matra* time. The symbol of prolonging notes for *meend* without dots are accepted as [⌢] and for combined notes as [⌢].

In the Indian Music system there are a number of taal variations which are not used in western music. Not only this, western music uses the taal with evenly spaced numbers only but in Indian music we have a number of taals which are odd and very complicated to play and understand. The notation of these taals and compositions set to these taals are naturally very hard to grasped.

There are a number of expressions such as 1.75 times of a beat, or .25 times of a beat, or 2.75 of a beat in Indian music notation system.

These expressions should be understood in Indian system only and be mastered in order to have a better command over the music of any form.

Part – 3
Know The Tanpura

Various Types of Tanpura

The look of the tanpura has gradually changed from the time it originated. Today, the tanpuras have different looks according to variety. It varies a lot on the basis of its size, look, decoration and on the basis of where it is manufactured. This is an instrument used both in Hindustani and Carnatic music. According to its uses, depending on who is going to use it, whether a male or female, a vocalist or instrumentalist, there are different kinds of tanpuras. Its size also vary according to the choice of the player.

There are three kinds of tanpuras:

1. Male Tanpura: The Tanpura used by male performers all over the world. It has its own unique features which differentiates it from other tanpuras.

2. Female Tanpura: The Tanpura used by women performers all over the world. It has also its own unique features which makes it different from other Tanpuras.

3. Instrumental Tanpura or Tamburi: An altogether different tanpura. It has its own features that gives it its place in the field of music and among musicians. The foremost feature of this is its portability and size. That is why it is called Tamburi, instead of a Tanpura. It is known by other names such as Tamburi, Tambua, etc, in different parts of the country.

Apart from this we can differentiate tanpuras according to their manufacture, size and style also. Now, we will explain each type one by one.

Male Tanpura:

This type of tanpura is used by male singers only. The sound production of this type is its low pitch. The length of this tanpura is slightly more than the other tanpuras. The total length of the male tanpura is fifty-seven inches, the width of the soundboard is seventeen inches, the circumference of the gourd is fifty-four inches and the length of the neck is forty inches. This is the size of a standard male tanpura. Male vocalists pitch their tonic note (Sa) to the first black key of the piano, C#. But depending upon the scale of the singer it could be tuned to a higher scale also. The male instrument has an open string length of one metre.

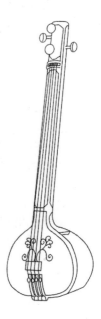

Female Tanpura:

This type of tanpura is used by women singers only. This is slightly shorter than the male tanpura. The sound production of this tanpura is high pitched compared to that of the male tanpura. The female voice has low pitch and high frequency hence this type of tanpura is best suited for the female voice. The length of a female tanpura is fifty-one inches, the width of the soundboard is fifteen inches, the circumference of the gourd is forty-eight inches and the length of the neck is thirty-six inches. Again depending upon requirement the female tanpura can be tuned to a slightly higher scale.

Instrumental Tanpura:

These small tanpuras have become very popular because they are easy to carry from one place to another and also sound good. These types of tanpuras allow greater range of scale in which they could be tuned. The instrumentalist uses different range of scale depending upon the sound quality of the instrument and the scale in which it sounds best. Generally the instrumental tanpura is three or four feet long and other specification varying according to the choice of the artist. This type of tanpura is sometimes fitted with additional string that give support to the instrumental recital. Unlike bigger tanpuras, they do not contain a hollow gourd but a solid sphere of wood. Instrumental tanpuras are gradually becoming popular among musicians.

These days there are electronic tanpuras too, which do not require a player to play it. These are being preferred by most of instrumentalists. The original tanpura is so beautiful that it cannot be compared to the electronic one.

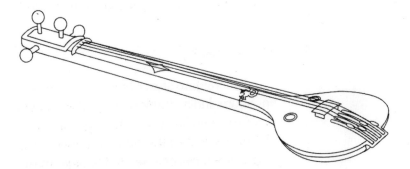

According to its manufacture style there are three different kinds of tanpuras:

1. Miraj Style

2. Tanjore Style

3. Tamburi

Miraj Style:

Miraj is a place in India best known for the best quality tanpuras. This type of Tanpura is especially famous for its sound quality. Miraj style of tanpuras are simple in construction and do not contain any decoration. This enables Miraj tanpuras to resonate sound well. This type of tanpura is most popular among performers of Hindustani music or North Indian music. Both men and women artists use this type in their performances. The round lower chamber to which the sound board is fixed is actually a selected and dried gourd. This gourd is responsible for the resonance of sound.

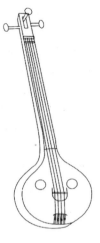

Tanjore Style:

The Tanjore style of tanpuras are made in South India. Tanjore is a place in the southern part of India which is known for the production of this type of tanpura. This is a tanpura mostly used in Carnatic music. It has a somewhat different shape and style of decoration from that of the Miraj style. The Tanjore tanpura's neck tapers towards the top. Its front plate is extremely flat. Also the Tanjore style tanpura does not have carvings on it. Its lower part is a solid wooden sphere instead of a hollow gourd. The neck is somewhat smaller in diameter. Since this Tanpura does not have carvings on it, it reflects the sound very well and produces a very rich tonal quality. Again, both men and women artists of Carnatic music use this type in their performances.

Tamburi:

This type has gained popularity recently due to its small size and portability. Apart from this its sound is most suited for the instruments. It gives the desired drone effect and at the same time does not kill the drones of the instruments itself. It is two or three feet long. It may have four to six strings. The small five-string tamburi are tuned to the higher octave and are the preferred instruments for providing the drone for solo-performances by string-playing artists, as the lighter, more transparent sound does not drown out the lower register of a sitar, sarod or sarangi.

Parts of a Tanpura

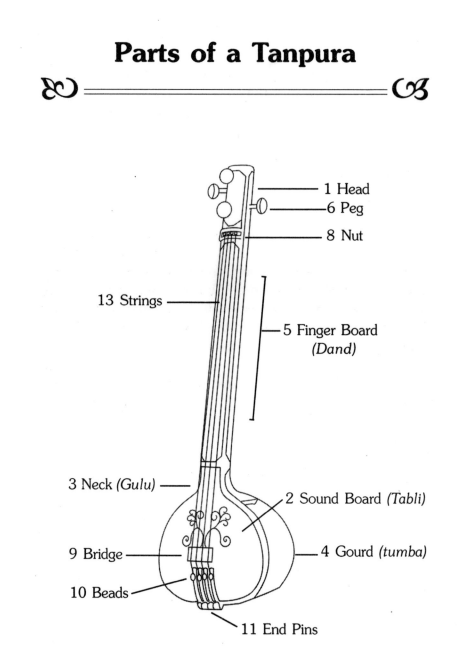

1 Head

6 Peg

8 Nut

13 Strings

5 Finger Board
(Dand)

3 Neck (Gulu)

2 Sound Board (Tabli)

9 Bridge

4 Gourd (tumba)

10 Beads

11 End Pins

Parts of a Tanpura

ೞ ════════════════════════════ ಐ

In the previous chapter we have seen the various types of tanpuras. Let us now look at the anatomy of the tanpura and see what are the components that make a complete tanpura. We will discuss about the different parts of a tanpura and see how they function. We will try to understand the work done by each component.

1. **Head**: The top portion of the finger board is called the head. On the Head the strings are attached the pegs firmly. This is a single wooden piece attached to the lower wooden piece of the finger board.

2. **Sound Board(*Tabli*)**: It is a kind of wooden plate of Tun-wood fixed on the top of the *Tumba* (Gourd). It is the main part of the tanpura that produces the sound. The thickness of the soundboard effects its quality of sound.

3. **Neck(Gulu)**: It is a small piece of Tun Wood in the shape of a neck. It joins the gourd *(Tumba)* and the finger board *(Dand)*.

4. **Gourd(*Tumba*)**: It is a big dry pumpkin which is hollow inside. The one prominent feature of the tanpura. It is made after selecting one from many chosen pumpkins. This is used as a resonating chamber.

5. **Finger Board (Dand)**: Although the tanpura is a fretless instrument and its finger board is not used to produce sound, it is important, as this is the place from where the strings pass over and produce sound when gently strummed.

6. **Pegs(Gatte)**: The pegs are used for tuning the strings of the Tanpura. They are normally made of *Shisham* or Teak wood. These pegs are fixed in the holes of the *Dand*.

7. **Silk or Cotton threads (Tandi)**: These threads are used to fine tune the strings to produce that particular buzzing sound effect for which the Tanpuras are known for.

8. **Nut (Tardan)**: It is an ivory piece fixed on the upper part of the *Dand*. Cuttings are made according to the number and size of the strings. Strings are first passed over the nut and through the hole of the adjuster container and tied to the pegs. Keeping the nuts clean for a hassle free passage of the strings through it, is mandatory.

9. **Bridge (Javaris)**: This is the most important part of a tanpura. The principle of javari can be likened to the prism's refraction of white light into the colours of the rainbow. It is its acoustic twin. The bridge is made of ivory. The overtones of the tanpura are produced by the vibration of the strings against the bridge.

10. **Beads (Manka)**: These are made of ivory or bone and used specially for fine tuning the tanpura. It is done to tighten the string by moving it forward or back. It passes through both the Bridges placed on top of the sound board. The top or the bigger bead is placed on top of a wooden Bridge. The Bead is placed between the bridge and the end-pin.

11. **End Pins (Kelli)**: These are ivory pins or sometimes metal pieces fixed to the Toe of the Tanpura. It is on the end-pins that all the strings of the Tanpura are tied. It holds the pressure pulling force of the strings. Its firmness is very important, otherwise the pull will break the gourd of the Tanpura.

12. Rosin (chalk): The common chalk is a vital part of a Tanpura. It helps in the smooth movement of the pegs. Due to atmospheric conditions or change in humidity level, the pegs may become too tight. Applying a little chalk by rubbing the pegs smoothens them so that they work perfectly.

13. Strings (*Tar*): Generally there are four strings in the Tanpura but sometimes a fifth or sixth string maybe attached by some players. Out of these some strings are made of steel and some of bronze. These strings vary in size and thickness and thus produce different sounds when plucked. These are the strings that are responsible for the production of sounds as there are no frets or any other means to manipulate sound.

✻ ✻ ✻ ✻

Making of a Tanpura

The Tanpura is a simple hand-made instrument which does not require any special technical know-how. The making of a Tanpura is as simple as the instrument itself. Tanpura making is an individualised art or craftsmanship. The instrument is made by seasoned craftsmen. Wood is the prime material used in a Tanpura. Apart from wood, some other things are implied but basically all other articles used are mainly derived from nature itself. Although, machines are not used in this process some technicalities are involved in making a Tanpura. What is described here maybe considered only a sample of how a Tanpura is made. Like most individual crafts this has also been passed down from one generation to another. An apprentice learns from the older seasoned craftsman who knows the art or craft. It is a manual craft not machine made. Simple hand tools are generally used in making a Tanpura. These are hand saws, rasps, hammers and similar tools. Power tools are generally not used. Glues, paints and varnishes used are usually made from scratch.

The Tanpura is a Hindustani musical instrument made from a special dried gourd which is further treated to enhance its durability. The basic structure of the Tanpura consists of a base *(tumba)*, which is a hemisphere-shaped, hollowed gourd. This gourd is selected from large sized pumpkins. These pumpkins are grown for this purpose alone. The gourd is selected from these pumpkins and treated to suit the purpose. The gourd is thickened with a process known to the craftsmen. A semi-rounded long wooden structure is then attached to the base and its upper flat surface functions as the finger board. This wooden block is selected from seasoned wood such as Teak or Mahagony.

The gourd and the wooden block in combination makes the body of a Tanpura. There are tuning pegs fitted to the front end of the instrument. These tuning pegs are an important part of the instrument as they hold the strings and are responsible for the tuning of the tanpura to the desired note. Small rounded beads are used to fine tune the strings to adjust the microtonal variations in tuning. But remember there are so many things that has to be kept in mind before a Tanpura is made. The length of the neck and the diameter of the gourd all decide the tonal quality of a Tanpura. The maker, according to the choice and demand of the musician, decides the length and all other specifications of the instrument. Not only this, the tone of the instrument also depends upon the polishing of the bridge. This bridge needs to be polished at regular intervals to ensure a better tonal quality always. Although it is not very complicated a seasoned craftsman can only bring out the required tonal quality, hence it is somewhat technical in nature.

The fasteners used in making a Tanpura are not metallic nails. Metal is hardly used in such types of instruments as it can tear away the wooden base or any part of the instrument. Screws are sometimes used but the most common fastener is a small tack or nail made from slivers of bamboo. There are scores of these bamboo nails on the inside. The largest nail used in the Tanpura is the end pin to hold the strings. Apart from this, no other major metalic screws are used.

For decoration some wooden carvings are made on the body of the Tanpura. It has something to do with the tonal quality of the instrument also, but it is done primarily to only add beauty to the looks. The Tanpura without carvings reflect the sound well and therefore these types have better tonal quality. Some artists use the instruments without carvings for their good resonance and tonal quality. Apart from this, varnish is also used to polish the outer surface of the instrument to give it a shine and glaze. It is again an important aspect to note that too much varnish could dampen the sound of the instrument. Therefore, proper attention must be given to the polishing of the instrument.

Thus, although simple in making, the Tanpura is not so easy to be made by anyone. Only a specialist can do this. At present seasoned craftsmen are decreasing day by day but still there are a few who have stuck to their ancestral craft and are busy doing what their older generation did and promoting the prestigious heritage of our culture.

✻ ✻ ✻ ✻

Part - 4
Playing The Tanpura

Sitting Positions

There are a few different proper sitting positions for this instrument. Especially for women, there are sitting positions that are appropriate and recommended by cultural norms of the Indian society. For men there is no real restriction except that the tanpura should be held to enchance the looks of the performing group.

For illustration, we give some recommended sitting styles that are generally used in the traditional music system. Some of these sitting styles are common for male and female while some are exclusively for male only. Try these postures and choose the one which best suits you.

Position 1: Traditional Indian Male Style

This style is recommended for male artists, although there is no restriction for women who adopt this style. In this style the Tanpura is kept resting on the shoulder. The gourd of the Tanpura is kept on the lap and the fingerboard rests over the right shoulder. Keeping the right hand over the strings strike the strings gently with your fingers. Pay attention that the Tanpura is kept steady and not allowed to rock, move or weave as this can be very  disruptive to the visuals of a performance. This style is very useful if the artist himself is playing the Tanpura in a concert. Otherwise, the accompanying artists can also sit like this as it looks nice on the stage.

Position2: Traditional Indian Style

There is another prominent posture recommended for artists. It could be well adopted by both men and women. Keeping the right leg lifted up from the knee and raised to support the Tanpura in front of you while the left leg stays on the ground. This posture is again very comfortable and widely used in concerts. This style is generally adopted by the accompanying artist who play as a support artist to the main artist.

Position 3: Traditional Indian Style

This style is exclusively adopted by the male only. In this style of sitting the Tanpura rests on the floor. The artist sits by the side of Tanpura and plays the strings with the fingers. In this style the artist is free to move his legs backward or forward occasionally to avoid the tiredness due to many hours of sitting.

Important Tips While Playing the Tanpura

Now that we have the sitting postures for playing the Tanpura it is up to you to select any of them according to your desire and convencience. Keep the instrument in the proper way according to your posture choice. Now there are some important tips to follow while playing the tanpura.

TIP 1

Take a deep breath and concentrate on the center of your cerebrum. This is spiritually addressed as the "ISHT" or God. The general idea is to bring the active side of one's thinking around to the emotive side of the "Naad" sound coming suggestively from the tanpura's drone.

TIP 2

Hold the instrument with the right grip, the arm on the gourd and the fingers on the finger board. Concentrate on yourself and be ready to play.

TIP 3

Now gently try to sing the OM sound on the tonic note Sa. Sing the vowels in a long, elongated period of time, without getting breathless. Repeat this process as many times as you can.

TIP 4

In the beginning the voice might falter. Try to remove the wavering which comes naturally in the voice. Gradually your vocal muscles will be accustomed to it and with regular repetitions the sound will be firm with the tone without cracking or getting out of tune.

TIP 5

When your voice is well set, start adding other consonants or different notes according to the *Raga*. Gradually improvise the notes according to the permissible rule and movement of the *Raga*.

TIP 6

You can sing to a whole octave or a part of it. It is up to your discretion. Relax and carefully concentrate on bringing emotional effect to your voice.

TIP 7

After obtaining a little confidence you can add another tone, such as Re, Ga and so on. Make sure you connect the "Re" as you strike the 5th note "Pa" of the Tanpura. This interval should harmonize perfectly.

TIP 8

Normally the **first** and **second fingers** are used to play. They should hold the strings gently and be relaxed. Always remember the central idea of the Tanpura is to control the oscillation of the voice at will and release it when required, without straying from the actual tone.

Part - 5
Sounds

Playing Technique

The Tanpura is not an instrument to give solo performances with. It is only a supporting instrument and its main function is to provide the basic drone or the "*Aadhar*" note. Based on these drone notes the artists improvises the *Ragas*.

Prior to playing, the Tanpura should be well tuned otherwise it will sound discorded and give an unpleasant sound. Initiallly the tuning may seem to be difficult but it is not so difficult. Although it takes some time to be able to recognize the variations in microtonal notes. With a little practice sufficient mastery could be achieved in tuning the Tanpura. Playing the tanpura does not require any special skill. You just have to strike the strings in a proper manner to a specific rhythmic structure. The soft part of the finger tips are used to strike the strings to produce a sonorous and sweet-soft sound. It should be struk in a continuous repetitive manner to create a musical hallow all around. It should be noted that harsh and tough strokes can distort the sweetness of the sound, hence striking should be in a soft manner. Apart from this the sequence of strking the strings should also be maintained. It should be first strings first and thereafter second, third and fourth and so on.

Now we will learn the following playing techniques. These are:

1. **Strike Sequence**

2. **Hand positioning**

3. **Rhythm of striking**

4. **How to Pluck**

Strike Sequence

Once you are comfortable with the sitting and holding posture and the instrument is stable in your hands, place the thumb of your right hand on the right side of the long shaft somewhere close to the middle. Strum the strings in a sequence Pa/Sa/Sa/Sa. This will depend upon the tunning of the instrument based on the notes of the raag. But start from the first string first and thereafter moving over to the second, third and fourth. Start with the middle finger on the first string and follow it with the index finger playing the next three remaining strings.

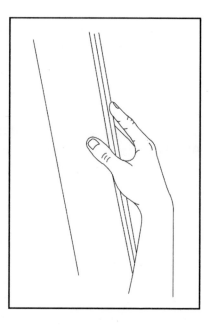

Do not strike the strings harshly. This can generate jarring and disproportionate overtones. Instead be gentle. Strike the strings with the soft pad of the tip of your middle and index fingers. As it slips and releases the strings, it produces a soft reverberant tone. This will make the sound clear with a mellow and rich timbre. It will also blend will with your voice. Let each string reverberate while you strike the next in a slow deleberate manner. One more thing is to be kept in mind, and that is, the rhythm of playing should be maintained. The striking should be balanced and continuous.

Positions of Hands and Fingers

The basic aim of the tanpura is to produce drone notes in a continuous manner rich in overtones as possible. For this, the thumb is positioned in such a way at the neck of the tanpura and the fingers are placed not across but if possible parallel to and approximately over the centre of the strings. There is no fixed and defined way as to where to keep the fingers on the string. But keeping the sound quality in mind, one should play accordingly. Keeping the

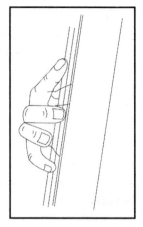

fingers close to the bridge will produce a metallic sound. So it should be a little away from the bridge

How to Pluck the strings

Now, a new player or beginner will be confused as to how to strike the strings. In the described position the first string is plucked with the middle finger, the second, third and fourth with the index finger, one after the other. The strings are plucked with the soft part of the finger tip and the action itself is more like striking or rolling of the strings than actually plucking them. The stroke with the help of the soft part of the fingertips gives a very smooth sound which is very refreshing and

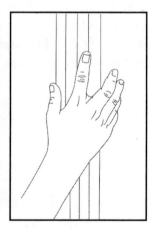

complete. Playing in such a way, the strings will sound soft without producing a striking or build up noise. With regular practice one can achieve the skill for striking the strings. Here we have to take note that the striking should be in a rhythmic structure. Pluck the strings one at a time, in a steady, repetitive, almost orderly manner as directed.

Rhythm of Plucking

A regular rhythm is kept to every string struck in approximately the same tempo, except the fourth will have some time to fade away. The rhythm is not monotonous, machine-like or metrically fixed but a free floating organic vibration.

Conclusion

The sound of the tanpura is for Indian Music like the earth for us humans. She carries us away most of the time without us noticing it. Every movement we make within the bounds of her gravity, she defines our understanding of space. If she has too many cracks or rocks we stumble and move only with difficulty. We are tied to her and at the same time she is our base for excursions into infinity.

Part- 6
Tuning the Tanpura

Tuning

We require a good tuning aesthetic to make the Tanpura sound sweet and impressive. For this we should have a basic instinct to understand the notes and its lesser variations. In Indian Classical Music, even micro-tonal notes are of very great importance. Therefore, before learning how to tune a Tanpura, adequate attention should be paid to the understanding of these micro-tonal notes and the basic notes.

We have Tanpuras with different number of strings attached to it. There are tanpuras with four, five or sometimes six strings. Here below is the tuning method of every Tanpura with different number of strings attached to it.

There are two basic tunings to consider - Sa/Pa and Sa/Ma. Tanpuras with 5 or more strings are allowed some creative tuning possibilities.

The choice between the two is made by the *Raga* that is to be performed. *Ragas* such as *Bageshwari*, *Malkauns*, *Abhogi*, *Gunkali*, etc have the fourth as a *Vadi* or *Samvadi* hence has a strong inclination to the Sa/Ma relationship. But other *Ragas* as *Todi*, *Kalyan*, *Puriyadhanashri* etc. with *Vadi* notes Dha *komal*, Ga, Pa, etc will require the Sa/Pa tuning.

Then there are *Ragas* that don't have a fourth or a fifth in its progression, like the *Raga Marava*. Here the third is a good choice.

Certain *Ragas*, like "*Pooriyaa*" of *Marvaa Thaat*, have the seventh note Ni (*Nishadha*) as the *Vadi*. Here the note maneuvers end up on the lower Ni and the vocalists might choose to tune the *Pancham* string to this note.

When the instrument is completely tuned you are ready to start your vocal practice. If you like, you can even give the tanpura to another player, who can sit next to you or behind you during a performance or practice.

4-stringed tanpura:

The standard tuning for 4-stringed tanpuras consists of the fifth, octave and tonic. Some traditional options for that purpose are given below. As an alternative to the traditional solutions many creative musicians make up their own tunings. These are the possible tuned notes :

First Method: Tune the first string of the Tanpura to the Pancham (Pa) of the middle octave. The second and third strings are tuned to the Sa of the middle octave and the fourth string is tuned to Sa of the lower octave, such as :

Pa - Sa - Sa - Sa

If Pa is not allowed in any particular raaga then the first string is tune to Madhyam (Ma) while the rest of the strings remain the same as mentioned above:

Ma - Sa - Sa - Sa.

If there is a raaga in which Ma is either not allowed or less important then the tuning could be as follows:

Ni - Sa - Sa - Sa, or

Dha - Sa - Sa - Sa

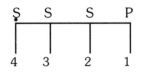

5-Stringed Tanpura:

Some Tanpuras contain 5 strings. The tuning method of such tanpuras is a little different, although the basic principle is the same.

The standard tuning for 5-stringed tanpuras with different possible alternatives is as given below:

Pa - Sa - Sa - Sa - Sa

Ma - Sa - Sa - Sa - Sa

Ni - Sa - Sa - Sa - Sa

Dha- Sa - Sa - Sa - Sa

Pa - Ni - Sa - Sa - Sa

Ma - Ni - Sa - Sa - Sa

Ma - Dha - Sa - Sa - Sa

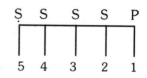

For example, in the first case, the first string is tunned to Pancham or Pa, the second string to the middle Sa, the third and fourth strings are tunned to the middle octave Sa while the fifth string is tunned to Sa of the lower octave to create the drone.

Similarly, in the second case, the first string is tunned to Ma, if Pa is not going to be used in the *Raga* or is less important. the second, the third and fourth strings are tunned to the middle octave Sa and the fifth string to the Sa of the lower octave.

By the method explained above, it is clear that only the first important note is changed according to the notes of the *Raga* while the remaining arrangements remain the same.

6-Stringed Tanpura:

Some Tanpuras contain 6 strings. Again the tuning method of such tanpuras is a little different, although the basic principle remains the same.

The standard tuning for 6-stringed tanpuras with different possible alternatives is mentioned below:

Pa - Sa - Sa - Sa - Ṣa - Ṣa

Ma - Sa - Sa - Sa - Ṣa - Ṣa

Ni - Sa - Sa - Sa - Ṣa - Ṣa

Dha - Sa - Sa - Sa - Ṣa - Ṣa

S Ṣ S S S P

6 5 4 3 2 1

For example, in the first case, the first string is tuned to Pancham or Pa, the second string to the middle Sa, the third and fourth strings are also tuned to the middle octave Sa and the fifth string is tuned to Sa of the lower octave to create the drone.

Thus, according to the method discussed above, the tuning arrangements can be changed according to the notes being used in the *Raga*.

Tips for tuning Tanpura

One may be confused initially when tuning a Tanpura as it is a bit difficulat to diversify between the two notes. As a ready reference some important tips are below to assist the player in the initial level of tuning.

TIP 1

Make sure that the two middle steel strings are tuned perfectly. Even a slight difference in intonation can be very distracting.

TIP 2

Choose a key in which you are able to sing to, which is within two and a half octaves. If you have a piano, harmonium or other keyboard use them as reference. If nothing is available, buy a good electric tone generator or a shruti box (drone keeper), preferably one aligned with international tuning standards. This will help you in future recordings or performance projects.

TIP 3

Strum each string and check its intonation with the reference tone. If any of the strings need further adjustments turn the pegs slowly while getting the feel of the tone. Use the main pegs to approach close to the note but always try to do the final fine tuning by using the beads. Stop when the result is satifactory and move on to the next string.

TIP 4

One thing should be kept in mind with all accoustic instruments is that a tuned instrument can change unpredictably. Temperature, moisture, just lifting the tanpura, or simply tuning an adjoining string can cause a change. Ideally one should fine tune the instrument before performing.

TIP 5

When all the four strings are set, check the *Jawaari* threads again and try to optimize the resonating sound.

TIP 6

The threads of the Tanpura is of vital importance. Use these threads to slide below the strings over the *Jawaari* to produce that very buzzing sound, typical of a Tanpura.

These are few important things that should be kept in mind when tuning the Tanpura. These few simple steps if followed attentively will help to tune it better. Initially, it might be confusing but it is not so. With a little practice, you can master this art as well.

Part- 7
Maintenance of
Tanpura

Repairs & Maintenance of Tanpura

With a little care and precaution the Tanpura can be kept in perfect working condition for a rather long time. A little knowledge of repairing the minor problems of the instrument is required of every player. With this knowledge, the instrument will be ever ready for use. When repairing the Tanpura the following can be done easily by the player himself to keep the instrument in good working condition:

(i) Replacing strings and

(ii) Polishing the top of the Bridge for a clear sound of the strings.

Replacing the Upper Strings

First of all remove the string you want to replace from the instrument. Thereafter, take the string of equal or to the length desired. For this, you can measure the length by placing the strings from one end to the other. Make a hook at one end of the string and attach this hook to the end pin. Hold the other end of the string and take it to the tuning peg. Pass this other end over the bridge and ivory nail. Attach it to the tuning peg by inserting the string into the hole of the peg meant for this. Now tighten the string by rotating the pegs and tune the string to the desired note. Initially, the string may slip but after a while it will firmly grip onto the peg.

Polishing the Top of the Bridge

It is often seen that with constant playing, there are some kind of scratches made on top of the bridge. These scratches make the instrument dull. Hence it requires polishing. To do this loosen the strings and clean the surface of the bridge with a zero number sand paper or file.

It is important here to give the proper shape to the bridge of the Tanpura. Although this is a work of a specialist but a player also can do it.

Maintenance of the Tanpura

(1) The instrument must be protected from extreme weather conditions.

(2) When not in use the strings must be amply loosened to prevent it from being torn off.

(3) If it is to be kept in a corner, place it in a plastic or cotton cover in a standing position with the front facing the wall.

(4) To Keep the Tanpura safe, a wooden box duly lined with cotton sheet or velvet cloth may be used. This protects it from weather changes.

(5) When transporting the instrument from place to place without a box, hold it firmly between the right arm and the side of the chest, holding the finger board with the right hand. Keep the gourd backward to protect it from getting hit.

Tips for Buying a Tanpura

ॐ ══════════════════════════ ೞ

When it comes to buying a Tanpura we are often unsure and don't know which to select. Any buyer can be confused by seeing the many designs available and may be deceived by the seller into buying an inferior quality instrument for the price of a superior one. The following points will help when purchasing a tanpura.

TIP 1.

Normally a new buyer is attracted to the beauty of Tanpura but remember that it is the sound quality, and not the appearance that is important. A buyer should note the tonal quality of the instrument. The sound should be round and sweet.

TIP 2.

The quality of wood used in the Tanpura is very important. One with seasoned wood should be preferred to normal wood only because this type of wood is resistant to the effects of weather and lasts longer.

TIP 3.

The accessories used in the Tanpura should be of considerably good quality. Such as the beads and the *mankas* which should be of ivory, for a longer life.

TIP 4.

The Price is another aspect to be kept in mind. Initially a cheaper Tanpura will do because there is chance of wear and tear in a new hand. Later on when one has mastered the art, a new and better quality could be purchased.

Notes

Notes

PANKAJ PUBLICATIONS

Suggested Readings on Strings Instruments

Learn to Play on Sitar

ISBN: 81-87155-14-0

A Best-seller book of the popular 'Learn to Play series', talks about Learning the worlds' favorite instrument in detail. Pictorial details of handling, postures and tuning the instrument for the comfort of every learner. A sure pick for the advance learners.

Sitar - Learn & Play

A Detail book on Sitar Learning with colored pictures explaining positions, postures and playing. The book is available in both HINDI & ENGLISH language. A series of exercises are given for practicing advance techniques of sitar playing. Comes along with an audio C.D. Explaining sounds of sitar.

Learn to Play on Violin

ISBN: 81-87155-46-9

A Best-seller book of the popular 'Learn to Play series', talks about Learning the worlds' favorite instrument in detail. Pictorial details of handling, postures and tuning the instrument for the comfort of every learner. A sure pick for the a learner.

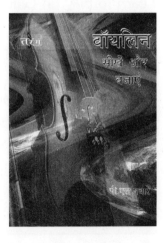

Violin - Learn & Play

Hindi   - ISBN: 81-87155-90-6

Book in HINDI & ENGLISH languages explaining the techniques of learning and playing the Violin like a pro. Color pictures with detail explanation.

PANKAJ PUBLICATIONS

Learn to Play on... Series

Book Name	ISBN
Learn to play on Tabla Vol-1	81-87155-00-0
Learn to play on Tabla Vol-2	81-87155-01-9
Learn to play on Harmonium	81-87155-22-1
Learn to play on Flute	81-87155-33-7
Learn to play on Sitar	81-87155-14-0
Learn to play on Violin	81-87155-46-9
Learn to play on Veena	81-87155-47-7
Learn to play on Guitar	81-87155-15-9
Learn to play on Mouth Organ	81-87155-03-5
Learn to play on Bongo-Congo	81-87155-68-X
Guitar Chords	81-87155-16-7
Indian Dances for Beginners	81-87155-02-7
MIND OVER FINGERS	81-87155-80-9
Distinction! in Music Theory Exam	81-87155-94-9

For Information or to Order,

Please visit our website: **www.pankajmusic.com**
or Email us at: contact@pankajmusic.com
or simply write to: **Pankaj Publications, 3, Regal Building, Sansad Marg, New Delhi - 1100 01.**